Sid and Zak

Written by Nicola Sandford
Illustrated by Jess Mikhail

Zak is at Sid's.

Zak has got a man.
"My man is Ozz."

Sid has got a man.
"My man is Quest."

Zak tells Sid,
"Ozz is the boss!"

Sid yells at Zak,
"No, Quest is the boss!"

Ozz runs at Quest.

Biff! Boff! Bonk!

Quest drops.

"Yes! My man wins!
He is the boss," yells Zak.

But Quest gets up!

Quest zaps Ozz.

"Yes! My man wins.
He is the boss," yells Sid.

"No, I am the boss and stop the din!"